How to Make Money as a Kid

Caleb Maddix

Table of Contents

CHAPTER 1
The Opportunity

Wwwwhat's up Maddix Addicts? Before we start off, let me ask you a question. Do you want to make money as a kid? The other day, I was with a kid I was mentoring, and I asked him, "Do you want to make money?" He replied, "What? What are you talking about Caleb? Of course, I want to make money." He is just like us. We all want to make money. We want to be able to buy any toy as soon as we want it. We want to be able to buy something for our friends and show off how cool we are because we worked hard and made our own money. We want to be able to get our dream car when we turn 16 years old.

But let's consider the other option. Let me ask you another question. What would your life be like if you grew up and didn't have any money at all? If you were to get to your 16th birthday and had to get a really crappy car, or maybe you couldn't even afford a car? How would you feel then? What about if you must work for a boss, that doesn't even care about you, in a job that you don't even care about, and they're bossing you around all the time so that you can just make enough money to eat? What kind of life would that be?

We don't want to work at a job we hate. We want to be able to do unbelievable things and not even have to worry about money, because we have so much of it. We want a really nice house. We want to buy the clothes that we really want. We all want to make money! If you disagree with these statements, then you might as well put this book down now. But if you're anything like me, and like most kids, we want to make money. In order to do that, there's some things that we are going to have to do.

In this book, we are going to talk about how to be more like that first case scenario, and have the money, rather than being stuck in the second case scenario. The sad thing is that most adults out there are in the second case scenario. They are doing jobs they hate, following the system, being "normal, and being average. So, whilst they're being average, we are going to be savage, and make money as a kid.

Now the first thing you may be thinking is, hang on Caleb, I'm just a kid. Can't I think about making money when I'm older, or isn't there some shortcut, or maybe even is it possible for me to make money now? Well to that, I'll tell you this, we live in 2017. We have the greatest opportunities, and we are blessed, with the opportunity of a lifetime, to be able to live in this era. No matter how old you are, you can do what you love doing and make thousands of dollars doing it. In some cases, millions of dollars doing it!

Look at me! I'm just some kid who wants to make an impact, who writes books, who does videos every single day on social media, who is growing a business, and currently I've made $200,000, and I'll probably be a millionaire by the end of this year. Let me give you another example. Take Emil; He started a lawn mowing company at nine years old. You know what he thought? I want to make a $1,000, so he got started. Now his lawn mowing company has literally made him over $100,000 in just one summer, and he's now making millions of dollars. That's what you can do in today's market.

Maybe if we were living 100 years ago, it would have been acceptable to do a job that we didn't like, or it would have been expected that we live a life that we didn't 't want to live and not make a lot of money. In 2017, we have choices and it's unacceptable to not be making money doing what we love doing. Here's another example of what we can do; Just look at EvanTube. At eight years old, he started the YouTube channel called EvanTube. Now he's making approximately, big word there, approximately $1.3 million every single year.

You are probably wondering what his videos are about? How is he making so much money? His videos are literally about stuff like Mine Craft™, Angry Birds™, and Lego™. Now I know there's a lot boys and girls out there, who love Mine Craft, Lego, and Angry Birds. You might even be thinking, but I could never do that. I can never make money off this. This is just a waste of my time. However, the reality is you can make money off things like that. You can make money doing anything, just doing the things you are passionate about.

If you like singing, you don't have to wait until you're older. There are now stars who start off singing on apps like Music.ly™. If you like doing comedy, you don't have to wait until you're older to get an acting role. You can be like Jake Paul and start posting funny videos. He now has over 19 million followers and makes millions of dollars. Look at someone like Mikaila Ulmer, she sold her lemonade company to Whole Foods for $1 million.

Kids, 60 years ago there were people starting lemonade stands all over the place. It was atypical way that kids could earn some money. But, because we live in 2017, and because we have the opportunities to make money, we can do exactly the same stuff our parents did, but make millions of dollars from, it. We can make money by doing all the stuff that we love doing; playing video games, hanging out with friends, doing funny stuff, making people laugh.

With this book, I am going to share with you how to take this opportunity and run with it. This opportunity means we can make money doing what we love doing, and not grow up being broke, hating our job. We are going to take that opportunity and use it wisely. It all starts in the next chapter; Let's get started.

CHAPTER 2
The Wall

I used to be just like you. I wanted to make money, not the hundreds of thousands of dollars that I'm making now. I just wanted to make my first thousand dollars. I thought it would be unbelievable if I could make $1,000, so I started trying. I started selling stuff, started trying to make money, but I never actually made money. I would go out, I would try and sell, I would do all the stuff I'm going to tell you about in Chapter 7. I thought I knew how to sell. I had listened to all these successful people tell me how, but I wasn't making any money. Even the times when I did make money, whether it was from a sale or someone gave me money, it always felt like I would lose that money immediately afterwards. Maybe I'd buy something I shouldn't have or the money just got away from me.

I realized that I had hit a wall. Later, I would learn that this wall was made of self-limiting money beliefs. What's a self-limiting money belief? It is something that limits yourself from making money. The more that I look back at that time, I realize that there were 10 things that I was struggling with when it came to money. I want to share with you how I smashed through this wall.

The 10 things you need to know about money, so you can make money.

There are 10 things that you need to know about money which, when you do them, will mean that you can hop right across that wall and be rid of those self-limiting money beliefs, and make money

1. The world runs on money.

The first thing that you need to know about money, is to understand that the world runs on money. You see, I heard a lot of people tell me, "Caleb, money isn't everything." "Caleb, you shouldn't be focused on money." "Caleb, the world doesn't revolve around money." I heard all this different stuff and then I started seeing millionaires. I started seeing billionaires. I started seeing the way that they think about money. I started thinking for myself, and instead of just believing what people had been telling me, I realized that, even though people say money isn't everything, everything in the world actually runs on money.

I mean, think about it ... I asked people, "Okay, if money is not everything, then what is everything?" They would say stuff like "Giving is everything". Now I totally agree with that however, it's very hard to give and to make a big impact without having money. I thought about all the things that make me happy, all the things I like. You know what? If I want to get a toy, that costs money. If I need to go to the dentist, that definitely costs money. If I want to get new shoes, that costs money. If I want to eat, that costs money. So, if money isn't everything, then we would all starving to death because the only way to get food is to pay for it.

2. You make more money when you do what you love.

The second thing that I learned about money, that helped me overcome my wall, was that you make more money when you are doing what you love doing. Now, we're going to be talking more about this later in the book, where I am going to share a story that really proves this point. A lot of people say that the safe route to earning money is getting a job, or the safe route is doing something that you don't want to do. You may even hear people say: "You know, sometimes you just got to do what you got to do to make money." The truth is, the riskiest route is to not do what you love doing. Jim Carrey said, "You can fail at what you don't love so you might as well go after what you do love." That's very true.

But think about those kids who are going to grow up without the guidance of the information from this book. They're going to get a job that they will probably hate doing. How much money do you think they're going to end up making? I mean, if they do really well, they might make tens of thousands of dollars a year, but then you look at someone like EvanTube. He's just eight years old, and what he loves doing right now is playing Minecraft and video games testing out toys, and he's making more money than the average person who's not doing what they love doing. It wasn't until I accepted the fact, that I would never actually make money until I was doing what I loved to do, that I actually started to make massive amounts of money.

3. Wealthy people are not bad.

The third thing you need to know about money is that wealthy people are not bad. I used to hang out with my friends and I would hear them say all the time, "Oh, look at that guy. He thinks he's really special. He's so full of himself, driving that expensive car," or, "Wow, He's super rich. He gets everything handed to him." People talk badly about money or wealthy people, but the truth is the more you focus on other people's wealth, the less wealth that you can actually have for yourself. In order to avoid this, I make sure that I never talk badly about anybody but I especially don't talk badly about successful or wealthy people.

Let me give you an example. If I saw someone wearing nice shoes in my class, I would never say, "Oh, he really thinks he's something special" I would say, "Nice shoes, man. How'd you get those?" or, "You know, you have great parents for buying you those" or, "What are you selling to be able to have those shoes?" It's all about perspective and understanding that wealthy people are not bad. The truth is I've met more wealthy people that are good, and doing good things than those that are bad.

If you look at someone like Bill Gates, he's worth 86 billion dollars and he's given more away to charity than 99% of the world put together. Do you think that makes him a bad person? Do you think he's all that just because he has money? Do you think he's greedy because he has money? I think it's better if you're wealthy. I think you can do more for people.

4. You deserve to be wealthy.

The fourth thing that I learned about money is that you deserve to be wealthy. I used to always think; "I don't know if I can actually make money. I don't really deserve it," or, "I'm too young," or, "I wasn't really taught the right stuff," or, "I'm not the best in school."

I made up all these excuses as to why I didn't deserve to be wealthy instead of doing the things that would make me deserve to be wealthy. You need to understand that every person, regardless of who they are, or where they live, deserves to make money. Anybody who truly loves what they do, and follows the steps inside of this book, will make money. They will become wealthy.

5. Money is your friend.

The fifth thing I learned about money is money is your friend. Lots of people have a bad relationship with money. They think badly about money, or they play around with it, or they disrespect their money but you need to act like money is your friend. You need to be best friends with money. Here's an easy way to do this; I always make sure that I have money in my pocket. Think of it in this way. Who do you hang out with the most? Your friends. Who are drawn to you the most? Your friends. As soon as you go to school, who comes up to you first? Your friends. So, if you develop a strong friendship with money, then money will come to you the most. Every time that you're in a situation, money is going to come to you.

What do friends do? They hang out with their friends a lot. They talk to their friends. Everywhere they go, they're talking or thinking about their friends. It should be the exact same way with money. Everywhere you go, you should have some money on you so you can feel it. For me, I like to do this thing where I sniff money. I just smell it and say, "You know what? I make more money. I deserve money. I deserve to be wealthy." It's all about developing a good friendship with money.

6. Money only comes to those that respect it.

The sixth thing is that money only comes to those who respect it. When I started out the number one problem that I had with making money was the fact that, at that time, I didn't respect it. There was this one time my dad and I were driving down the highway going really fast. We had the windows rolled down, you could feel the wind, and hear the loud music that my dad had blaring from the stereo. I don't remember where we were going but we were super excited. Inside one of the cup holders, there were four quarters. I was about eight years old at the time, I picked up one of the quarters, had it in my hand, and then I threw it out the window. Suddenly, my dad got super serious.

He looked me in the eye and said, "Caleb, why did you do that?" At first I was like, "Dad, it's only a quarter. It doesn't matter? It's a quarter. You can get them anywhere." My dad said, "It's not about the quarter. We don't technically need that quarter but it's the fact that you disrespected money. You disrespected it." He looked at me and said, "How you treat that quarter is going to be how you treat a million dollars. How you treat anything is how you treat everything." He said, "If you disrespect that quarter, that means you disrespect money. If you disrespect money, money will never respect you and money will never come your way" What you need to learn is to develop a good relationship with money and respect it.

7. Your wealth is determined by who you hang around with.

The seventh thing you need to know about money is your wealth is determined by who you hang around with. I was hanging around with a lot of people who have a poverty mindset. Poverty means to be poor but it's more than just not having money. It's okay to hang around people who don't have money but it's not okay to hang around those people who have a poverty mindset, and who don't have a good relationship with money. I was hanging out with people who thought badly about money. They would always make fun of wealthy and successful people, and it started to rub off on me. They were definitely not following the 10 things I'm talking about in this chapter.

I decided to start hanging out with wealthy people, to start going to networking events and meeting and talking to as many wealthy people I could, learning from them, and reading their books. From the moment, that I started hanging round with them, the more money started coming to me. I love this quote; "If you're in a room with five millionaires, you're going to end up becoming the sixth millionaire. The reason is you become who you hang around with." Remember, a ship never sinks from the water outside of it but only from the water that gets inside of the ship so make sure you're careful who you let inside of your ship.

8. Money listens.

Number eight is that Money listens. I used to say stuff like I'm broke, or I don't have money. What I realized is that the more I said I'm broke, the more money listened to me. The more I said I couldn't make money, the more money listened to me. Money listens to the things that you say. If you say over and over that you're broke, then money is going to be like, "Okay, you say you're broke, you're not going to have any money." However, if you start saying stuff like, "I'm wealthy. I deserve wealth. I'm going to impact millions of people with my wealth. I'm going to be worth over one million dollars." When you start saying more positive stuff like that, money is going to listen, and respect your request. What I want you to start doing every day is to say; "I deserve wealth. I am wealthy. I'm one of the wealthiest kids on the planet." Once you start saying it, money will start to listen.

9. Money goes to those who deserve it.

Number nine is that Money go to those who deserve it. When I was trying to make my first thousand dollars, I remember that I kept hoping for a short cut. I kept hoping that someone would just walk up to me on the street and hand me a thousand dollars. What I realized is that money won't come to anyone who doesn't deserve it. So, I asked myself, "If someone is going to make a lot of money, what did they do to deserve it?" The simple answer to that question is that they work hard. At that point I said to myself, "Man, I can't keep looking for shortcuts or for a magic pill. Instead, I'm going to work for what I want." I started going out, doing things and taking steps towards my goal, even if it was things I didn't really want to do. I did the work. Money realized that I deserved it and it came to me.

The person who deserves to be the wealthiest is going to be the wealthiest. You don't deserve what you desire. You deserve what you do. A lot of people think, I deserve to be wealthy because I want to be wealthy.

Wrong! You might want to be wealthy, but you deserve to be wealthy when you take action, read books like this one, and apply the things that we're talking about.

10. You should want a lot of money.

The tenth thing you need to know about money is that you should want a lot of it. People used to be constantly telling me, "Caleb, you shouldn't want to be a millionaire. That shouldn't be your focus." The truth is every kid should want to be a millionaire. Some people say, "Caleb, I don't want to be a millionaire. I just want to be happy."

Why do you have to choose? Why not want to be happy and want to be a millionaire? The good news is you can go for both. You can be happy. You can make money. You can make a difference. You can have it all if you go after it, if you work hard enough, if you apply the things I'm telling you, and if you deserve it all, you will have everything you want, so make sure you want a lot. Dream big! The reason that I've made hundreds of thousands of dollars, maybe even millions by the time you're reading this book, is because when my friends were shooting for $10 for lunch money, I was shooting for $100,000 for my future.

After working through and applying these 10 things, my wealth started to grow. I broke through my wall of self-limiting beliefs. I went from knowing that there's an opportunity, knowing that there's a wall, to breaking through that wall and making the money that I've made today.

Now, that you understand the basics, you have the foundation in place that you need to deserve wealth, and for wealth to want to come to you. In the next chapter, we're going to talk about actual action steps that you can take to not only want and deserve money, but to actually get money. I'm excited. Let's get into "The Money Formula"

CHAPTER 3
The Money Formula

So, in the last chapter, we built our foundation. And in this chapter, we are going to start building on that foundation.

I was speaking at an event in San Diego, and I was networking with lots of people. I found out that a guy in the audience was worth $500 million. As soon as I heard this I immediately ran to the back of the room, shook his hand, and for about six to seven hours straight I just picked his brain and wanted to learn. I want to learn from the best and you should to.

At the very end of the conversation, he finally gave me the secret of how he made over $500 million. He said that the answer to his success was a book by Napoleon Hill called "Think and Grow Rich." He said that every time he read that book, he made a million dollars. I worked it out, he's read the book over 500 times. So, I asked him, "What would be the one thing you would take from this book, if you were only allowed to know one part of the book? And he told me there were five steps.

I want to share these five steps with you, but it's important that you not only listen to what I'm saying, but that you also apply these steps. I'm going to give you the five-step money formula but you need to put it into action.

The Money Formula:

Step One: How much money do you want to make?

This first question is one of the most important questions. Where many people go wrong is that they are not clear about how much money they are going to make. They will say things like, "I hope I make money" or "I want to make a lot of money" or "I want to be worth millions of dollars". The problem is that those are all very broad statements. They need to be specific.

In my experience, the people that I've met, that are worth millions, even billions of dollars, all know exactly how much money they want to make. I asked him, "How much money do you want to make?", And he told me the exact amount, right there right then. And it made me realize that if someone worth $500 million knows exactly how much money they want to make, then I should probably know exactly how much money that I want to make. If billionaires know exactly how much money they want to make, then I should know exactly how much money I want to make.

I was taking notes as he spoke, and I wrote out how much money I wanted to make.

Step Two: When do you want to make this money by?

The second thing he told me; "Caleb, the second step is the thing that will actually help you make that money. He told me to write down when I wanted to make that amount of money by. He stressed that it was important that I write more than just the date. He wanted me to write out the date, hour, and exact time that I was going to have this amount of money.

So, I did. I wrote out the exact time that I wanted to make the amount of money that I had written down. He did the exact same thing. He told me to the hour and minute when he is going to be worth a billion dollars. He knew it to the second and it makes a lot of sense to do that. Just think about it: When you have a school project and you have five weeks to get it done, 90% of the time you end up waiting until the last day complete it.

But let's imagine that there was no deadline. You don't know when you must hand it in. Do you think you would do that project? If your teacher said I want you to do this project but I'm not going to tell you when you have to turn it in, you can just do it when you feel like it. 90% of the kids in the class won't ever do it. I used to be one of those kids.

This reminds me of a project I had to do, I was probably in third grade, where I had to put together a book of pictures of mountain lions. I remember that I had three months to get this done. It was one of those projects that they gave you a very long time to do. So originally, I sat down and said, "okay I'm going to get this done in the three months." The problem was that I had no plan so the next thing you know it's two months and 29 days later I still haven't done my project. On that final day, I rushed around to get it done. My Mom and I went from store to store, looking at books, trying to find all the pictures that I needed. We did the entire thing in three hours.

But imagine that we had not had a deadline. That project would never have been done. It is really important to understand that "you are dead without a deadline". If you don't know when you want to make that money by, you will never actually make it. These steps will only work if you are crystal clear. So instead of saying I want a Lamborghini, be clear and say what type you want. I want this Lamborghini, this year it came out, this model, this color, this version, and I want to buy it here. Get that specific and then set the exact date, hour, and time that you are going to get it by.

Step Three: How much of this money are you going to give back?

The third step that he revealed to me is what you want to give back out of that amount of money. We're going to talk about giving back in chapter six, but this is still an important step for you to do here. First map out how much money you want to make, then map out when you want to make it by, and then ask yourself: Out of this money that I want to make, how much am I willing to give back? We've already talked about how money is an energy and that money respects people who are going to give that money to more people. Money likes to be circulated and touch the hands of as many people as possible. So, it will naturally flow to those people who are going to give it to others.

Write out the exact amount you want to give others. It could be to a charity, a homeless person or someone who needs it. Determine exactly how much you want to give. The $500 million man made me write it down and I did.

Step Four: Write your statement.

The fourth part of the money formula is to write your statement. I already had one, but you may not. I want you to write down how much money you are going to make, when you're going to make it by, and exactly how much you are going to give in return. It might look something like this: I want to make $1000 by April 24, 2018 at 6 pm and I want to give $100 of that $1000 to a single mother.

This is your mission statement. This is your thing that you are going to aim for. The $500 million man made me take that statement that I had, take a piece of tape, and as soon as I flew back to Florida where I'm from, he had me hang it up on the mirror. Every single time I go and brush my teeth, I would look at that statement.

Step Five: Say your statement out loud.

The final step that he told me was to say my statement out loud twice a day. So, whenever I'd go to brush my teeth, I would see it on the mirror and I would say my mission statement. And then at night when I was going to bed, I would say the statement again. This made me focus on my goal, and next thing you know, I started to accomplish it. And even today, I still do this. Since I met the $500million man following this money formula and it works.

Now it's not magic, it's not a short cut. However, if you take action, it will seem so simple. Sometimes it may not be easy to make the money, but it will be simple in the long-run because you're as clear as you possibly can be. Follow the advice that this $500 million man gave me, that I'm sharing with you today. Follow this five step money formula, and money will come your way. If you want to know how I made my first $1000. Keep reading, I reveal how I did it in the next chapter!

CHAPTER 4
How I made my first $1,000

U p to now, we've been throwing around pretty big numbers like $100,000, $1 million, $500 million, and even $1 billion. However most of you are probably just thinking, "Man, that's great, but even just making a thousand dollars would be unbelievable and would change my life. I could buy what I want. I would have freedom, and I would have the right base from which I could make much money." Don't worry, there is nothing wrong with you. It doesn't make you a bad person or mean you have bad money beliefs because you just want to make $1,000 or even $100.

You always have to find a place to start. I was in the same position about five to six years ago. I remember that I wanted to make $1,000. I thought, "Man, if I can make $1,000, then I can buy this, and I could do this, and I could order this." It seemed impossible and unbelievable, all mixed together, at the same time.

So, what changed? One day I was sat there and said to myself, "Enough wishing, Caleb. It's time to map this out. I am going to do the math." I made a decision and took action.

I sat down, pulled out a calculator and said, "Okay. If I sold 10 things at $100, that would be $1,000. If I sold 100 things at $10, that would be $1,000. If I sold one thing at $1,000, that would be $1,000." I mapped out the math behind making $1,000 and realized that selling 100 things at $10 seemed like the best way for me to make $1,000.

The next step was to write a list of everything that I could sell for $10. Let me give you an example, "I guess I could sell a painting for $10." I found someone in my class who could paint and draw really well and I said, "Hey, if you let me sell your painting for $15, I'll give you $5 and I'll keep the other $10, since I sold it." I ended up selling seven paintings, and that wasn't $1,000, but at least it made me $70.

The next thing that I decided to do was start to sell tea. I went out and I sold about 20 teas at $10, but then the sales started to slow down, so I looked for something else. "What if I sold erasers and I sold them for $5? If I sold two, that would count as $10." So, I started selling two erasers for $10. Next thing you know, I sold a couple of those and I had made money. I made over $500 just from doing the math, but I still hadn't made my $1,000 yet.

I asked myself, "What else can I do for $10?" Bam. It hit me. I could write a book for $10 and sell that. That's how I wrote my first book, Keys to Success for Kids. I started selling those, and I sold over 500 copies in the first few months, and that helped me make about $5,000.

Just simply doing the math helped me make that much money. However, then I was stumped; "$5,000. Cool, but how can I make $50,000?" I started trying to do all this different stuff but it wasn't working. I went back to what had worked before and did the math. I figured that, "If I sell this much of a $60 product, that will equal $50,000," so that's what I did.

I felt stumped again when I wanted to make $100,000. This time I went to Grant Cardone's office. If you don't know who that is, Grant Cardone is a New York Times bestselling author. He has a real estate company worth $500 million. He's extremely wealthy. He impacts millions of people and have millions of followers on social media.

I asked Grant Cardone, "Grant, how can I make $100,000?" He told me, "Caleb, the answer is on your phone." I said, "What do you mean, Grant?" I thought he was saying something sarcastic, like, "I don't know. Google it." but he said, "No. The answer to making $100,000 is right on your calculator on your phone." He said, "How many would you have to sell at what price to make $100,000?" I did the math once again, and I made $100,000.

Now my goal is to make $500,000, and I'm doing the math. My next goal will be to make a million, and yes, I'll be doing the math. Regardless of my target, $10 million, $100 million, even $1 billion, it will all follow the same process and that starts with simply doing the math.

I want you to do the math. Look at your statement, the one you taped to the mirror. Now think about the formula. How much money do you want to make? Now start thinking, "What can I sell? How much money can I charge and how many of those things can I sell in order to make the amount of money that I want to make?" Map it out and start selling that thing. It all starts with sales. We'll talk more about sales in Chapter Five but everything starts with sales.

I was hanging out with one of my friends, that I've known for a very long time, and she said to me, "Caleb, I just want to hurry up and get a job, so I can make some money," and I kind of laughed for a second. I asked her, "Okay, how much money do you want to make?" She said, "If I could make $13 an hour at a job, it would change my life. I would feel amazing if I did that." I said, "Do you have any job options that would help you make that much money?" She answered, "Yeah, but all three of the job options that I have, I really hate and I don't want to do," but then she said, "I guess that's what you have to do in order to make money nowadays."

I stopped her right there, as I could tell that she was going down the path of the average person. She wasn't being savage and was just being average and asking, "What job can I get?" I said to her, "Hold on, so all you want to make is $13. What's your passion?" She said, "I have a passion for making T-shirts and I would love to sell them," but then she said, "I guess you really can't do that until you're an adult. I'm just a kid." I kind of laughed and said, "Okay, what's stopping you from doing it when you're a kid? Why can't you do it now?" She started thinking and realized, "Ha. There's actually nothing stopping me."

I pulled out the secret weapon, which is doing the math, and said, "Okay, if you made a T-shirt, how many T-shirts would you need to sell to make $13?" She said, "If I sold two T-shirts, that would make me more than $13. It would actually make me about $20." I said, "So, if you went out and you sold two T-shirts every single hour, you would be doing what you love doing and be making $7 more than doing what you hate doing," She started thinking and her eyes opened wide up. "No way. That could actually work," To which I responded, "Of course, it will work, because we did the math." Just by simply shifting her from her mindset of trying to make money and putting her into the mindset of doing the math and simplifying it, she could make money.

It's time to stop thinking that you must do something you don't like doing in order to make money, because if you do the math and simplify it, you never know how much money you could end up making.

So, time to act. Write out how much money you want to make. Do this math, and the only math you'll be doing in the future is counting how much money is in your bank account.

CHAPTER 5
My Dad's Last Words

It was my dad's 40th birthday and we were in Gatlinburg, Tennessee. We took the cover off the hot tub. It was pretty cold so you could see the steam rise from the hot tub as soon as the cold air met the heat. We got in and started chatting about how cool my dad's life had been up to his 40th birthday and what his goals were for the next 40 years of his life. We had great fun talking about the memories that we'd already made, and the memories that we were going to make together in the future. But there was one question that night that changed everything for me. I asked, "Dad, if you were going to die right now what would your last words to me be?" He replied, "Caleb, if I was about to take my last breath I would tell you this."

I assumed he was going to say something like, "Stay positive, work hard, never give up, read, eat healthy, give." But all the thoughts that started rushing through my mind at that moment, just froze in their tracks as soon as my dad said these two simple words, "Master sales." That's right, if my dad could only leave me with a couple final words, they would be master sales. This threw me off balance, I was confused, and I had to ask my Dad, "Why? Why, if these are your last words, would you say master sales?" He said,

"Because if you know how to master sales you can do anything. You will never have to worry about money, or about making a difference in the world. You'll never have to worry about your future if you know how to sell."

I knew what my Dad was saying was true, but I didn't understand it as much as I do now. The more that I've gone through in my own life, the more people I've met and the connections I've made with the wealthiest people on the planet and with the kids that make the most money, I've noticed they all share one skill. They know how to sell. There are examples everywhere. The best athletes in the world, have to sell the crowd that they're the best. Top musicians are selling their music at every performance. Even the most popular religions must sell what they think is the truth to their followers. No matter what goal you are trying to accomplish, you must know how to sell, not just how to sell things to make money, or how to sell your talent to the world, but in much smaller ways.

We've been selling to our parents since we were babies. Our version of selling was to cry and cry, until our parents either held us, changed our diaper, or gave us food. Making friends is just selling strangers the idea that it would be a good idea for them to hang out with us every single day. Whether we wanted to go on a vacation or we wanted a new toy, we had to sell our parents or grandparents on why they should buy it for us or why they should take us somewhere special.

The truth is that if that you only take one skill away from this book, it would be to master sales. In the last chapter, I'm going to share with you 21 ways to make money as a kid, but all of them are about sales and the art of selling. If you know how to sell, you can sell anything. You will never have to worry about money because even if you were to make a lot of money and then lose it all, you could start over by selling something. That's why I am certain that I will never be homeless because even if I have no money, I can always go out and sell some of old stuff or I could buy some things cheap somewhere and sell them at a higher price somewhere else.

There are so many different ways to make money, if you know how to sell. Remember it's not just about getting people to give you dollars; if you want to get into a top college, you are going to have to sell the admissions people on why they should let you attend their school. Let's say that you want to become a basketball player. You're going to have to sell your coach on why they should let you be on the team and play you in the games.

If you are still not convinced that mastering sales can help you in any situation, let me prove it to you. There was an event that I wanted to go to. It was in San Francisco and they wanted me to speak but I didn't have the money to fly all the way there and speak, so I asked my dad. I begged him over and over. "Dad, why can't we go? Dad, can we please go to this event? Can we please do this?" He looked at me, and said, "Okay, we can go but only if you raise the money that it's going to cost to get there."

I thought, "Okay, that doesn't seem too bad." I asked how much it would cost and he said, "It's $1,500." That stopped me in my tracks, I was shocked, "What? $1,500? That's more money than ... that's a lot of money. There's no way that I'm going to make that." My dad said, "Caleb, I taught you how to sell so let's go and put your skills into action." I went back to the math, "Okay. How much time do I have to make this?" He said, "You have 12 hours to make $1,500." Now, my dad did have the money, and he could have easily paid for it, but he was trying to teach me a lesson that when you don't know what to do, do something, and that something is sales.

So I did the math. I said, "Okay, I need to make $1,500. What's the easiest way for me to do this?" I realized the easiest way for me to do this would be to sell 15 things at $100. I decided I would create some sort of product. What I created was a product that basically taught older people how to use social media in the right way. I created the product, and I posted it on Facebook. I messaged people and asked them to share my post on their walls. For four hours straight all I did was promote the course, and then all these people reached out to me saying that they would like to learn about social media. I got on the phone with those people, I talked to them, and they would say stuff like, "You're just a kid." They would say all kinds of different things, sometimes they were mean but, because I knew how to sell, I ended up selling my $100 product to 20 of those people.

Not only did I get to go to San Francisco and speak at the event, but I also walked away with an extra $500. How I did it, all comes back to sales. It all comes down to when you don't know what to do, and you want something, you don't just hope it will happen or wish for it, but you sell to get it.

Let me give you another example, when I wanted something really badly. My dad and I were eating at the food court in the mall and I could see the Apple store nearby. I was about nine years old at the time and I kept thinking to myself, "Man, I really want an iPhone. I wish so much that I had a phone, I could play games, text my friends, call people, post on social media, and do all this stuff. The only way that I can do that and have that much fun is by getting an iPhone." I started hoping for it, I started wishing for it, but I knew that if I wanted something, I needed to sell to get it. So, as we were sitting there eating, I came up with the genius idea of trying to sell my dad on getting me an iPhone.

I looked at him directly in the eye and said, "Dad, what's stopping you?" I stared him right in the face. I had a ton of confidence. I made sure my posture was good. I eliminated all distractions that he had, and I looked at him and I said, "Dad, what's stopping you from getting me an iPhone?" He said, "You know what? I like that confidence." He said, "Sell me on it." So I did. "Dad, if I had an iPhone then I could use that access would mean that I could impact more kids than just trying to talk to them face to face. I'd be able to make more of a difference. Not only that, but whenever I'm at mom's house, I'd be able to call you." I went through my entire sales pitch and my dad ended up saying, "Because you tried to sell me and you didn't just hope for it, I am going to get you the iPhone."

We walked right into the Apple store and bought a beautiful, black, sleek iPhone that I wouldn't have had if I didn't know how to sell. The lesson from this chapter is you need to learn to how to sell, to get what you want. If you are in a bad situation, you can always sell your way out of it. You need to master sales.

Remember, don't hope for it, sell for it!

CHAPTER 6
What to do with your Money

All right, so now I've given you the tools. Now you know how to make thousands, even millions of dollars. The next question is, what to do with this money? Now, for many of you, the first thing you will do is have lots of ideas as to what to do with the money. You'll want to buy this and do all these different things. You will have all these ideas of how you're going to spend your money, however that not actually what you should be doing with your money.

You see, whenever I made my first few hundred dollars, I would spend it right away. Which meant that I was back down to zero dollars. It's different now, because my dad taught me this formula and I've also heard it from many millionaires and billionaires. It took me from making money and then losing it, to making money and then that money making me more money. My money works for me, and makes me more money. Because of that formula, I continue to make more and more money.

The formula is "Ten, Ten, Ten, Seventy". Here's how it works:

The first "Ten"- Save

Every time you make money, the first thing you're going to do is put ten percent into your savings. You're going to save ten percent of that money. Think of it this way. I learned this from one of the kids I worked with. What would you rather have? A million dollars today or a penny that doubles every single day for the next thirty days?

Obviously, you think you'd rather have a million dollars over a penny, right? The truth is, if that penny were to double every day, so the first day it becomes two pennies. Then it becomes four pennies. Then it continues to increase. By the end of thirty days, that penny would've turned into three million dollars. The question is, what would you rather have? A million dollars or three million dollars?

It's the same thing when you are saving. If you make a thousand dollars and you save a hundred of those dollars, then you're able to keep that hundred dollars and it will continue to grow. You may not want to save that money right away, but it's important to start creating good habits if you want to keep making more money.

To date, I've made hundreds of thousands of dollars and I've been able to keep the majority of it because I continue to save. All billionaires and millionaires save, they don't spend all their money right away.

The Second "10" - Give

The second "ten" in the formula is that you need to give the next ten percent of your money away. Let's say that you make a hundred dollars. You are going to save ten percent (the first ten) and then you are going to give ten percent (the second ten).

That means that as soon as you make a hundred dollars, you go out to the homeless or to someone who's poor or anybody you see, and you're going to give someone ten dollars. The reason for this is that impact is more important than income. Giving is more important than actually making money. Money, like I said before, is only going to reward those who give it away, so get into the habit of giving ten percent away.

The Third "10" - Invest

As the third "ten" you are going to invest ten percent of your money. A lot of people save and there are lots of times that people give their money away. However, what most kids, and a lot of adults don't understand, is that you need to invest part of your money back into yourself. If you made a hundred dollars selling lemonade, then out of that hundred dollars, you're going to take ten dollars and you're either going to invest it into someone promoting your lemonade stand or invest it into more supplies to make lemonade. You're investing it back into your business so you can make more money.

But why should you invest? When you make an investment, you're going to get something out of it. Put money back into your business, back into your product, and it will continue to grow. If you just make a whole bunch of money and don't invest, then you're going to end up being broke.

The Final "70" – Spend

Now here's the good part, after saving, giving, and investing, you get to spend! The fourth thing that you're going to do with your money is spend "70" That's right, I want you to spend seventy percent of your money. Well honestly, I'd rather you didn't spend seventy percent of your money. It's probably better if you spend forty or fifty percent of your money, but the truth is, you've earned it.

If you make a hundred dollars, then you can spend up to seventy dollars on whatever you want. Because you still have the thirty percent that you saved, gave, and invested so you are going to continue to make money.

Let's think big! Imagine you just made your first one hundred thousand dollars. Time to follow the formula – 10,10,10,70. You are going to save ten thousand dollars and you are going to give ten thousand dollars away. You're going to invest ten thousand dollars back into your business and you are going to spend seventy thousand dollars. Now you're not actually going to spend that much, but make sure you treat yourself to something you really want. After all, you worked hard for that money and we all have things we really want.

Those are the four things you need to remember to do with your money. Save, Give, Invest, and Spend. Follow these four easy steps and you will not only make money, but you will keep and make more of it.

CHAPTER 7

20 ways to make more money

I've now shared with you everything you need to know in order to make money as a kid. You know the Money Formula. Your money beliefs are all working for you. You know what to do with your money, once you've made it. You know how to get out of any situation through selling.

I want the last chapter of this book to be super practical. I asked some kids what was the one thing that they wanted to see in this book? They all wanted a list of practical ways to make money as a kid. So, that's what I'm going to give you, 21 ways to make money as a kid. Just remember that these are just ideas, you should make money doing what you love, so if your passion isn't on my list, go ahead and think about how you could make money doing your favorite thing. Even better, share your success story with other kids. Your idea may help someone else follow their dream.

Do not just follow this list because I wrote it. Do not follow any of the 21 things I'm about to tell you, if they are not what you love doing. Follow your passion. If you like singing, get out there and sing. Do you like playing sports? Start a YouTube channel around sports. Go with what you love. Do the math and figure out how you can make money doing that thing.

Let's get into the 21 ways to make money as a kid.

1. Sell your old stuff.

Most of us have things around our house, or toys that we got from Christmas, or birthday gifts from our grandparents that we never use and they're just sitting there. Get your parents' permission, and then go ahead and sell those old or unused things in a yard or garage sale or even just on the street. If your parents approve, this is a simple way to make money.

2. Sell water bottles.

What I used to do is buy a water bottle for 50 cents and then I would go and sell that water bottle for $1.20. I made a lot of money. I was selling about 30 water bottles a day and making a good amount of money.

3. Resell Things.

As a kid, I would buy something online, at a yard sale or from a friend, then I would sell it for more. Here's an example, I buy an item from a yard sale at $5. I would then sell that item for $8 and I would make $3 in profit. That was a simple way for me to make money. One time

I bought this thing from a kid at school for $50. That's sounds insane, right? Why would you pay $50 for something? But I could sell that thing for $124. That's $74 dollars profit on one sale. So, start buying items and then resell them to someone else for more money.

4. Sell paintings and drawings.

This is one of the number one ways that I started in my business. There was a kid in my class who was really good at drawing, so I used to get him to paint and draw all this stuff. I talk about this in Keys for Success for Kids 2.0. Once he had drawn stuff, I would go sell it for $20 and I would give him $7 and keep $13 dollars as my profit.

5. Hold a bake sale.

A lot of you are good cooks. You could make cookies or cupcakes and go around your school, church or other event and sell those things. My friends and I would have our parents make cookies and we'd sell them during lunch period at school. That was an easy way to make money.

6. Make food.

Similar to holding a bake sale, you can make other food items to sell. Some of you can cook, and most of you know how to microwave something. So, use your skills and make food that people want to buy. Maybe you can make some popcorn that you could go around and sell. All you have to do is figure out some sort of food that you're able to make or that your parents can make for you and then go sell that stuff.

7. Build a lemonade stand.

This is the very well-known thing to do for kids who want to make money. Ask your parents if they can make lemonade, or figure it out by watching a video on YouTube. Then build a stand and have people in your neighborhood buy lemonade from you.

8. Sell your talent.

This one that's is great for all of you that have a talent. Let's say that your talent playing the guitar. Why don't you go and play in public, and have people pay you whilst you play. You should look for a street where there are lots of people walking, e.g. the mall, theme park, market. You could do the same thing with singing or even drawing pictures. People pay whilst you sing or buy a drawing. Just think what am I best at? What do I love doing the most, and figure out how you can make money doing that.

9. Coach other kids.

When I was younger, I was pretty good at basketball, and there was a kid I knew who wanted to get better. He was about three years younger than me. I went to see his parents and said, "I will train your son in basketball, we can meet up once a week. I'll train him if you pay me $20." They were cool with it and they paid me. That was an easy way for me to make $20 doing something that I loved.

Coaching doesn't have to be limited to sports. You could tutor them in stuff for school or see if there's someone younger than you that you could help and give advice to and see if you can make money doing that.

10. Write a book.

This one is super important and definitely a good option for all of us kids out there. People are always blown away whenever you write a book, especially as a kid. I mean there's countless kids who have already written their own book, and who are making thousands of dollars off their books. I know one girl who read all of my books and decided to write her own book. Now, her book is now in every single school in Iowa. She's making money every school day and her book was turned into a movie. She gets to speak at all sorts of events and do all this cool stuff, but it all started with the book.

11. Start a YouTube channel.

This is also a great way for you to start making money. Start a YouTube channel, and once you're done with your videos or posts, then you could sell something at the end. That could be something you create e.g. your book or you can reach out to a local business and say, "Hey, I'll promote your business at the end of all my YouTube videos." There are so many ways to make money doing a YouTube channel, and it's a great way for you guys to make money, build up your confidence and start building your own brand as a kid.

12. Invent a product.

A lot of us have really good ideas and inventions that we can put together. Why not figure out some sort of idea or some sort of business then invent it and go sell that to people? Besides, it sounds pretty cool to be able to say that you invented something, right?

13. Do tasks for people.

This is very general, but it's true. Figure out what tasks you could do for people. What do adults need to get done, that you can do as a kid, that will save them time?

Then ask them if you can help them. Remember most adults want to support kids and give them money, so if you ask them with confidence, "What's stopping you from letting me do this, and you give me this much money for doing it," most of the time they'll say yes. It's a nice thing to do, and you will be making some money but it's also going to help you master sales and you'll learn a powerful worth ethic. This is a great way to make some money, and help other people.

14. Clean people's houses or cars.

People will pay to save themselves time, or from doing tasks that they hate. Get your parents' permission first but you never know how much you could make just moving boxes, cleaning out garages or washing cars. The key is to figure out how you could help someone with something that will save them time.

15. Mow lawns.

This is one of the classic ways for kids to make money. Remember Emil from Chapter One, who used to mow lawns. He ended up selling his lawn mowing company and making millions of dollars from the sale. But, he started out by doing these sorts of tasks for people.

16. Carry grocery bags to older people's car.

My dad used to have me do this, not only to make money, but also to teach me manners and respect. I would go to grocery stores and while older people were walking to their car and carrying their groceries, I would ask them, "Would you like me to help you with those?" They would say, "Sure," and they would hand me their bags. I would take their bags, and put them in their car, or if they had their bags inside of a cart I would push their cart, unload the bags, and then take the cart back for them.

I would then say, "Hey, I'm doing this to start off being a young entrepreneur. What kind of donation would you like to make for my service that I did for you today?" That taught me respect, it helped a lot of older people, and I made a lot of money off of it. A lot of older people would be like, "Wow, this kid has good manners. Let me give him a $20 bill." That was one of the best ways to make money and it taught me good manners and respect.

17. Do a car wash.

This is something you could maybe do with your friends to make some money. My friends and I wanted to go on a trip but we didn't have the money, so I organized a car wash. I advertised it and put it on social media so people would turn up. Loads of people came and paid us to wash their cars.

18. Shovel snow.

I live in Florida and it doesn't snow much here, but I know if I did live somewhere where it snowed a lot, this would be a really great way to make some money. A lot of people don't want snow on their driveway, but they also don't want to have to shovel the snow. So, you shovel the snow away for them and then charge them $20-$30. Jake Paul from Disney told me that this was how he got started, he used to shovel snow. If you want to be a millionaire like him, start shoveling snow!

19. Do projects for people on fiverr.com.

This is something you will definitely need to get your parents' permission for. There is a website called "fiverr.com", and basically people use it to get projects done for them. Go to the site, and look up all the categories and see if you have skills that fit in one of those categories. You'll need your parents to help you set up a profile on the site, there are YouTube videos that can help you with this. Once you have a profile, you put up the skill/work that you can do for people and they hire you. You can make a lot of money doing this if you have skills that people are looking for.

20. Get employees to sell for you.

This was the number one way that I made money as a kid. Although it is important for you to learn to master sales, it's equally important for you to sell people on selling for you. Let's say you decided to create drawings. That's a great idea from the list. But instead of having people draw and then selling them myself, I had four people in my class who would do the paintings and then I had 10 people in my class who would go and sell them. We would sell them for $20 to kids in our school, everyone wanted these paintings.

We would charge $20. I would give $7 to the person doing the drawings, I'd give $5 to the person who was selling it, and the rest was mine. This was a powerful way to make money, because I was making money even when I wasn't working, even when I wasn't selling. Start doing that and you're really going to succeed.